ENGINEERING ENDEAVORS:

A NAVIGATOR'S TOOLKIT

2

Contents

Introduction

The field of designing is a dynamic and steadily developing domain that assumes a vital part in molding the world we live in. From the wonders of current foundation to the mind boggling functions of state of the art advances, engineers are the planners of progress. As we leave on this excursion into the mind boggling and various scene of designing, this guide fills in as a compass, enlightening the ways to progress, offering bits of knowledge into the difficulties that lie ahead, and preparing trying and prepared designs the same with the devices they need to flourish.

Embracing the Intricacy of Designing

At its center, designing is about critical thinking, innovativeness, and advancement. Whether it's planning maintainable foundation, creating progressive advances, or enhancing complex frameworks, engineers are at the very front of tracking down answers for the world's most squeezing difficulties. The extent of designing is huge, including disciplines from common and mechanical to electrical and PC designing, each with its extraordinary arrangement of standards and applications.

The cutting edge engineer faces a dynamic and speedy climate, where progressions in innovation, changes in worldwide elements, and the consistently developing interest for supportable arrangements make a scene of the two potential open doors and difficulties. This guide is intended to be a buddy on this excursion, giving a far reaching guide to assist engineers with exploring the intricacies of their calling and remain ahead in a consistently developing world.

The Developing Job of the Architect

Designing isn't just about specialized skill yet in addition about versatility and a comprehensive comprehension of the world. Engineers now have to think about the ethical implications of their work, communicate effectively across diverse teams, and embrace interdisciplinary approaches because their role has expanded beyond traditional boundaries in recent years.

As we dive into the bunch parts of designing, from key abilities to cutting edge ideas, this guide stresses the significance of ceaseless learning and keeping up to date with industry patterns. Engineers are not simply issue solvers; they are visionaries, driving development and forming what's to come. This presentation makes way for the sections that follow, each offering important bits of knowledge and viable guidance for engineers at each phase of their vocation.

Exploring the Instructive Scene

The principal part of our aide brings a profound plunge into the primary strides of a designing vocation. Understanding the educational pathways and degrees available is essential when choosing a field of study. We investigate the assorted scope of designing disciplines, from the traditional common and mechanical designing to the state of the art fields of man-made reasoning and biotechnology. The significance of building areas of strength for an in center ideas is highlighted, laying the foundation for the specialized abilities that designers will develop all through their vocations.

Creating Fundamental Abilities for Progress

Past the specialized perspectives, effective designers have a bunch of fundamental abilities that rise above disciplinary limits. Section two spotlights on these abilities, going from capability with instruments and programming to the specialty of critical thinking and decisive reasoning. Powerful correspondence, both recorded as a hard copy and introducing, is a foundation of an effective designing vocation. Using time productively and project arranging abilities are likewise featured, as specialists frequently wind up shuffling various undertakings and cutoff times in the speedy universe of tasks.

The third chapter of The Journey of Professional Development delves into the subject of professional development, focusing on the significance of engineering community networking and the advantages of joining professional organizations. Nonstop learning is underscored, alongside the worth of accreditations in a consistently cutthroat work market. Engineers are urged to find some kind of harmony among individual and expert life, perceiving that a balanced individual is better prepared to confront the difficulties of a requesting calling.

Flourishing in the Working environment Climate

The working environment is a unique biological system, and part four gives experiences into exploring its complexities. From corporate culture and decorum to powerful group joint effort, specialists will track down viable exhortation on flourishing in an expert setting. Managing workplace issues and compromise techniques are essential parts of vocation achievement that are investigated top to bottom.

Dominating Undertaking The executives

Part five is committed to the craftsmanship and study of task the board. Understanding project lifecycles, establishing goals and milestones, budgeting, resource allocation, and risk management are essential skills for engineers who oversee projects from conception to completion. This section furnishes engineers with the apparatuses expected to oversee projects, guaranteeing productivity and viability in their work effectively.

Encouraging Advancement and Imagination

In section six, the aide investigates the significance of cultivating advancement and imagination in the designing system. Engineers are not simply issue solvers; they are likewise makers. Strategies, for example, conceptualizing and configuration believing are examined, alongside pragmatic ways to remain refreshed on industry drifts and arising advances.

Moral Contemplations in Designing

Designing choices have broad results, and part seven digs into the moral contemplations that architects should wrestle with. From sticking to proficient sets of rules to adjusting cost and wellbeing, natural and social obligation, and the significance of whistle blowing in instances of unfortunate behavior, this part gives a structure to moral dynamic in the designing calling.

Focusing on Wellbeing and Prosperity

A sound specialist is a useful designer, and section eight stresses the significance of wellbeing and prosperity in a requesting calling. Stress the executives, work environment security, and systems for keeping up with mental and actual wellbeing are investigated, alongside ways to accomplish a feasible balance between serious and fun activities.

Expecting Future Patterns

The last section looks towards the eventual fate of designing, investigating arising innovations, maintainable practices, the effect of man-made reasoning and mechanization, and the developing scene of remote work and virtual cooperation. Engineers are urged to embrace change and get ready for the difficulties and open doors that lie ahead.

Assets and Instruments for Specialists

The aide finishes up with two supplements. The first, Supplement A, gives an organized rundown of assets for engineers, including suggested books and distributions, online courses and instructional exercises, valuable sites and discussions, and fundamental devices and programming.

Glossary of Designing Terms

The subsequent reference section, Supplement B, incorporates a glossary of designing terms help both desiring and experienced engineers in exploring the specialized language that is characteristic for the field.

As we leave on this investigation of the designing calling, it is our expectation that this guide turns into an important asset for engineers at each phase of their professions. From the fledgling looking for direction in instructive decisions to the old pro adjusting to the consistently changing mechanical scene, "Designing Skylines" is intended to be a friend, offering experiences, functional counsel, and motivation for an effective and satisfying vocation in designing. Together, let us explore the difficulties, embrace the open doors, and shape a future where designing keeps on being at the front of development and progress.

Part 1: Beginning in Designing

1.1 Picking Your Designing Discipline

Setting out on an excursion in designing starts with a pivotal choice: picking your discipline. This part directs hopeful specialists through the plenty of choices, from the customary common and mechanical designing to the state of the art domains of man-made consciousness, biotechnology, and then some. Figuring out the unmistakable highlights, difficulties, and amazing open doors inside each discipline is foremost to settling on an educated choice that lines up with individual interests and vocation objectives.

1.1.1 Exploring Engineering Disciplines Overview of Major Engineering Disciplines

Specializations and Interdisciplinary Fields Emerging Disciplines and Technologies 1.1.2 Considerations for Decision-Making Personal Interests and Passions Future Job Market Trends Alignment with Career Goals and Objectives 1.1.3 Real-World Insights Interviews with Practicing Engineers from Different Disciplines Experiences of Professionals in Niche Fields

1.2 Educational Pathways and Degrees

After selecting the field of study, the next step is to This segment gives a complete outline of the different instructive ways accessible, including degrees, certificates, and concentrated programs. Figuring out the scholastic prerequisites and picking the right instructive establishment sets the establishment for an effective designing vocation.

1.2.1 Scholastic Certificates in Designing
Single men, Lord's, and Ph.D. Programs
On the web and Part-time Learning Choices
Proficient Affirmations
1.2.2 Choosing the Right Instructive Organization
License and Rankings
Industry Associations and Systems administration Valuable open doors
Research Valuable open doors and Offices
1.2.3 Exploring Difficulties in Training
Adjusting Scholastic Meticulousness and Useful Experience
Defeating Normal Instructive Obstacles

Tutoring and Direction

With the instructive way settled, this segment dives into the center ideas that structure the bedrock of designing information. Whether it's figuring out basic standards, numerical establishments, or the use of logical ideas, this part gives bits of knowledge into the fundamental structure impedes that plan engineers for the difficulties ahead.

1.3.1 Essential Standards in Designing

Mechanics, Thermodynamics, and Electromagnetics

Material Science and Properties

Liquid Elements and Intensity Move

1.3.2 Numerical Establishments

Math, Straight Variable based math, and Differential Conditions

Likelihood and Measurements in Designing

Computational Science

1.3.3 Pragmatic Utilization of Logical Ideas

Labs and Involved Learning

Certifiable Contextual analyses

Cooperative Tasks and Exploration Open doors

1.4 Exploring the Changing Scene of Designing Schooling

The finishing up piece of this part recognizes the advancing idea of designing training. It investigates the effect of innovation on learning strategies, the ascent of online instruction, and the significance of long lasting learning. Systems for remaining current with industry advancements and utilizing instructive assets for constant improvement are examined.

1.4.1 Innovation in Designing Schooling

Web based Learning Stages and Virtual Labs

Reproduction and Demonstrating Apparatuses

Expanded Reality (AR) and Computer generated Reality (VR) in Training

1.4.2 Deep rooted Learning Procedures

Proceeding with Schooling and Expert Turn of events

Industry Gatherings and Studios

Systems administration and Joint effort in the Advanced Age

All in all, Section 1 fills in as a primary aide for those venturing into the universe of designing, offering a guide to pick the right discipline, explore instructive ways, construct a strong groundwork, and adjust to the developing scene of designing training. To start a successful and fulfilling career in the diverse and dynamic field of engineering, aspirant engineers will find helpful insights and advice here.

Section 2: Creating Fundamental Abilities

2.1 Specialized Abilities: Apparatuses and Programming

Engineers are the planners of advancement, and this part centers around fostering the specialized ability fundamental for progress in the field. From dominating industry-explicit devices to remaining refreshed on the most recent programming patterns, designers will acquire bits of knowledge into developing the specialized abilities that characterize their skill.

2.1.1 Capability in Industry-Explicit Devices

Outline of Devices in Different Designing Disciplines
Involved Preparing and Studios

Accreditations for Apparatus Capability

2.1.2 Remaining Current with Programming Patterns

Significance of Programming Proficiency

Patterns in Designing Programming

Online Stages and Assets for Expertise Advancement

2.1.3 Functional Applications and Contextual investigations

Certifiable Undertakings Utilizing Progressed Instruments

Cooperative Programming Improvement

Critical thinking Through Mechanical Advancement

2.2 Critical thinking and Decisive Reasoning

Designing is innately critical thinking, and this segment investigates the craft of decisive reasoning. Designers will learn procedures to break down complex issues, settle on informed choices, and move toward difficulties with an imaginative and insightful mentality.

2.2.2 Creative Thinking in Engineering Importance of Creativity in Innovation Techniques for Generating Innovative Solutions Balancing Analytical and Creative Thinking 2.2.3 Real-world Case Studies Engineering Challenges and Solutions Success Stories of Innovative Problem Solving Lessons Learned from Failures

2.3 Communication Skills:

Writing and presenting ideas well are just as important as coming up with them. This section emphasizes the significance of having strong communication skills by covering engineering-specific written and oral communication strategies.

2.3.1 Specialized Composition

Composing Reports, Recommendations, and Documentation

Lucidity and Accuracy in Specialized Correspondence

Crowd Driven Correspondence

2.3.2 Viable Show Abilities

Planning Connecting with Introductions

Public Representing Specialists

Taking care of Inquiries and Difficulties During Introductions

2.3.3 Cooperative Correspondence

Group Correspondence and Coordinated effort Instruments

Distant Correspondence Procedures

Cross-disciplinary Correspondence in Designing Ventures

2.4 Using time effectively and Task Arranging

Designs frequently wind up shuffling numerous activities and cutoff times. This segment digs into the complexities of using time effectively and project arranging, offering methodologies to advance efficiency without settling for less on the nature of work.

2.4.1 Time Usage Systems
Prioritization Procedures
Putting forth Practical Objectives and Cutoff times
Defeating Tarrying in Designing Undertakings
2.4.2 Venture Arranging and Execution
Gantt Diagrams and Task Timetables
Asset Designation and Planning

Dexterous Task The executives in Designing

2.4.3 True Venture The executives Experiences

Interviews with Task Chiefs

Contextual analyses on Fruitful Venture Execution

Examples Gained from Venture Disappointments

2.5 Constant Improvement and Deep rooted Learning

In the consistently developing field of designing, the excursion doesn't end with a degree. This segment stresses the significance of nonstop improvement and long lasting picking up, giving architects techniques to remain ahead in their professions.

2.5.1 Embracing a Development Outlook

Developing an Outlook of Nonstop Learning

Gaining from Disappointments and Iterative Improvement

Looking for Input for Proficient Turn of events

2.5.2 Expert Advancement Open doors

Going to Meetings and Studios

Internet Learning Stages and Courses

Organizing for Professional success

2.5.3 Mentorship and Information Move

Significance of Mentorship in Designing

Coaching and Being Tutored

Information Move Methodologies inside Groups

All in all, Section 2 outfits engineers with the fundamental abilities expected to explore the difficulties of their calling. From specialized capability to powerful correspondence, critical thinking, and venture the executives, this part fills in as a thorough aide for fostering the diverse range of abilities that characterizes an effective designer. Architects will acquire functional experiences, certifiable models, and significant methodologies to upgrade their expert abilities and succeed in the unique universe of designing.

Part 3: Proficient Turn of events

3.1 Systems administration in the Designing People group

Building major areas of strength for an organization is a foundation of outcome in designing. This segment digs into the specialty of systems administration, giving techniques to laying out significant associations inside the designing local area and then some.

3.2 Joining Proficient Associations

Dynamic cooperation in proficient associations upgrades a designer's profession direction. This segment investigates the advantages of joining and adding to designing affiliations, social orders, and networks.

3.2.1 Choosing the Right Proficient Associations

Outline of Significant Designing Affiliations

Particular Social orders and Gatherings

Nearby and Worldwide Systems administration Valuable open doors

3.2.2 Contribution and Administration

Advisory group Investment and Volunteer Open doors

Serving in Positions of authority

Commitments to Proficient Distributions

3.2.3 Constant Learning Through Associations

Admittance to Industry Experiences and Exploration

Proficient Improvement Assets

Organizing Occasions Coordinated by Proficient Associations

3.3 Ceaseless Learning and Accreditations

In the quickly developing scene of designing, the obligation to persistent learning is non-debatable. This part investigates the different roads for progressing training and the meaning of confirmations in professional success.

3.3.1 Deep rooted Learning Techniques

Chasing after Postgraduate educations

Web based Learning Stages and Courses

Going to Studios and Short Courses

3.3.2 Expert Certificates

Perceived Certificates in Different Designing Disciplines

Advantages and Validity of Affirmations

Adjusting Work and Certificate Arrangement

3.3.3 Boss Supported Learning Projects

Valuable open doors for Manager Supported Instruction

Arranging Learning Advantages

Making a Customized Learning Plan

3.4 Adjusting Work and Life

Keeping a solid balance between fun and serious activities is significant for supported progress in the designing calling. This part gives experiences into techniques to accomplishing harmony between proficient responsibilities and individual prosperity.

3.4.1 The Significance of Balance between serious and fun activities

Influence on Mental and Actual Wellbeing

Upgrading Efficiency Through Equilibrium

Perceiving Indications of Burnout

3.4.2 Using time productively for Architects

Productive Preparation and Prioritization

Defining Limits and Overseeing Assumptions

Consolidating Relaxation and Leisure activities

3.4.3 Adaptable Work Plans

Arranging Adaptable Work Hours

Remote Work Potential open doors

Parttime and Occupation Sharing Choices

3.5 Exploring Profession Changes

Designs frequently face junction in their professions, and this segment tends to systems for exploring vocation changes, whether it be a change in discipline, industry, or job.

3.5.1 Evaluating Vocation Objectives and Yearnings

Reflection on Private and Expert Targets

Distinguishing Adaptable Abilities

Investigating New Open doors

3.5.2 Looking for Mentorship and Direction

Coaches in Profession Changes

Organizing for Progress Open doors

Proficient Improvement During Changes

3.5.3 Strength in Vocation Difficulties

Conquering Mishaps and Disappointments

Gaining from Profession Difficulties

Creating Versatility for Long haul Achievement

3.6 The Fate of Expert Turn of events

The closing piece of this part looks towards the eventual fate of expert improvement in designing. It investigates arising patterns, like customized learning ways, the coordination of computerized reasoning in training, and the advancing job of mentorship in the computerized age.

3.6.1 Customized Learning Ways

Versatile Learning Stages

Fitting Proficient Improvement to Individual Necessities

Gamification and Drawing in Opportunities for growth

3.6.2 Computerized reasoning in Schooling

Simulated intelligence driven Learning Stages

Prescient Investigation for Profession Improvement

Open doors and Difficulties of simulated intelligence in Proficient Turn of events

3.6.3 Developing Job of Mentorship

Virtual Mentorship in a Globalized World

Distributed Mentorship Stages

Consolidating Variety and Consideration in Mentorship Projects

All in all, Part 3 fills in as a complete manual for proficient improvement in the field of designing. Specialists will track down viable procedures for systems administration, joining proficient associations, ceaseless learning, balance between fun and serious activities, exploring vocation advances, and experiences into what's in store drifts that will shape the scene of expert improvement in the years to come. By embracing a proactive way to deal with proficient development, designers can situate themselves for progress and satisfaction in their dynamic and steadily advancing vocations.

Part 4: Exploring the Work environment

4.1 Corporate Culture and Decorum

Understanding and adjusting to the way of life of the work environment is vital for an effective designing vocation. This part investigates the subtleties of corporate culture and gives direction on working environment decorum.

4.1.3 Cultural Diversity and Inclusion Embracing Diversity in the Workplace Fostering Inclusivity Strategies for Effective Cross-Cultural Communication 4.2 Effective Team Collaboration Collaboration is essential to engineering projects. 4.1.1 Importance of Corporate Culture Defining Organizational Values and Norms Cultural Variations Across Industries Cultural Fit and Job Satisfaction

4.1.2 Navigating Workplace Etiquette Professional Communication Dress Code and Appearance In this segment, we dig into procedures for cultivating powerful collaboration, building positive working connections, and defeating normal difficulties.

4.3 Managing Workplace issues

Exploring workplace issues is an expertise that engineers frequently need to create. This segment gives bits of knowledge into understanding and overseeing office elements without compromising proficient honesty.

4.3.1 Perceiving Workplace issues
Distinguishing Power Designs
Exploring Casual Organizations
Adjusting Proficient Connections
4.3.2 Systems for Exploring Workplace issues
Building Partnerships and Organizations
Remaining Nonpartisan in Clashes
Overseeing Vertically and Descending
4.3.3 Keeping up with Proficient Honesty

Moral Contemplations in Workplace issues

Dealing with Moral Difficulties

Building a Standing for Trustworthiness

4.4 Compromise

Struggle is unavoidable in any work environment, and this segment offers pragmatic direction on overseeing and settling clashes expertly.

4.4.1 Sorts of Work environment Struggle

Relational Contentions

Task-related Clashes

Authoritative Struggles

4.4.2 Compromise Procedures

Undivided attention and Sympathy

Cooperative Critical thinking

Looking for Intercession and Outsider Mediation

4.4.3 Transforming Struggle into A valuable open door

Gaining and Development from Clashes

Reinforcing Connections Post-Struggle

Building a Positive Compromise Culture

4.5 Expert Development inside the Association

Propelling one's vocation inside an association requires key preparation and proactive commitment. This segment gives bits of knowledge into ascending the professional bureaucracy while contributing definitively to the association's objectives.

4.5.2 Professional Development Opportunities Training Programs and Skill Enhancement Involvement in Strategic Projects Pursuing

Leadership Roles 4.5.3 Navigating Hierarchical Structures Building Relationships with Superiors Effective Communication with Leadership Demonstrating Leadership Qualities at Every Level

4.6 Work-Life Integration Strategies

This section examines strategies for achieving a healthy integration of work and personal life, recognizing the importance of well-being for sustained career success.

4.6.1 Adjusting Work and Individual Responsibilities

Adaptable Work Game plans

Time Usage Methodologies

Family and Individual Needs

4.6.2 Pressure The executives Methods

Distinguishing and Tending to Working environment Stressors

Consolidating Pressure Help Practices

Looking for Help and Directing

4.6.3 Prosperity Drives in the Work environment

Boss Supported Health Projects

Emotional wellness Backing

Cultivating a Sound Work environment Culture

4.7 Adjusting to Changes in the Work environment Climate

The last piece of this part expects and addresses the unavoidable changes in the working environment, including mechanical headways, authoritative rebuilding, and worldwide movements.

4.7.1 Embracing Mechanical Changes

Persistent Figuring out how to Adjust to New Innovations

Tech Mix and Computerization in Designing

Expecting Future Mechanical Movements

4.7.2 Exploring Authoritative Rebuilding

Adjusting to Changes in Group Designs

Keeping up with Efficiency During Changes

Immediately taking advantage of Chances In the midst of Progress

4.7.3 Worldwide Elements and Social Variation

Exploring Worldwide Groups and Coordinated efforts

Adjusting to Social Contrasts in a Worldwide Working environment

Utilizing Variety for Development

Taking everything into account, Part 4 furnishes engineers with the abilities and procedures expected to explore the intricate elements of the work environment. From understanding corporate culture to succeeding in group coordinated efforts, overseeing clashes, and adjusting to changes, this part gives viable bits of knowledge to specialists to flourish and prevail in the different and dynamic scene of their expert climate.

Section 5: Project The board for Designers

5.1 Grasping Undertaking Lifecycles

This segment gives a primary comprehension of undertaking the board, underscoring the significance of exploring through various periods of a task.

5.1.1 Inception Stage
Characterizing Undertaking Goals and Degree
Distinguishing Partners and Task Group
Directing Plausibility Studies
5.1.2 Arranging Stage
Creating Undertaking Plans and Timetables
Asset Distribution and Planning
Risk Recognizable proof and The board
5.1.3 Execution Stage

Group Assembly and Undertaking Execution

Observing and Controlling Venture Progress

Correspondence Systems During Execution

5.1.4 Shutting Stage

Project Consummation and Expectations

Client and Partner Endorsement

Directing Venture Post-Mortems

5.2 Putting forth Objectives and Achievements

Compelling undertaking the executives requires clear objective setting and achievement ID. This part dives into the procedures for characterizing project targets and making practical achievements.

5.2.1 Specific, Measurable, Achievable, Relevant, and Time-Bound Goals in Engineering

Projects Aligning Goals with the Scope of the Project Communicating Goals to the Project Team 5.2.2 Milestone Planning Identifying Critical Milestones Creating Milestone Charts and Timelines Celebrating Achievements and Progress 5.2.3 Adapting Goals to Project Changes Flexibility in Goal Setting Reassessing Goals During Project Execution Communication of Changes to Stakeholders

5.3 This segment investigates techniques for planning, allotting assets, and enhancing monetary plans.

5.3.2 Resource Allocation Strategies Identifying Necessary Resources Balancing Workloads Among Team Members Adjusting Resource Allocation Based on Project Phases 5.3.3 Cost-Benefit Analysis

Assessing Project Costs Against Benefits Evaluating Return on Investment (ROI) Communicating Financial Metrics to Stakeholders

5.4 Risk Management

Every project comes with inherent risks. The best practices for project budgeting include: estimating costs and contingency planning; creating budget templates; monitoring and controlling expenditures; and Methodologies for identifying, evaluating, and mitigating risks throughout the project lifecycle are examined in this section.

5.4.1 Distinguishing Venture Dangers

Cooperative Gamble Distinguishing proof Methods

Making a Gamble Register

Characterizing Dangers In view of Seriousness

5.4.2 Gamble Evaluation and Prioritization

Quantitative and Subjective Gamble Evaluation

Focusing on Dangers In view of Effect and Likelihood

Making Chance Alleviation Plans

5.4.3 Persistent Gamble Observing

Standard Gamble Evaluations All through the Undertaking

Dexterous Ways to deal with Hazard The board

Correspondence Techniques During Chance Alleviation

5.5 Guaranteeing Viable Correspondence

Correspondence is the backbone of fruitful undertaking the executives. This part gives bits of knowledge into laying out clear correspondence channels inside the venture group and with partners.

5.6 Venture Documentation and Revealing

Exact documentation is fundamental for project achievement and information move. This part investigates the creation and upkeep of far reaching project documentation.

5.6.1 Undertaking Plans and Timetables

Creating Definite Undertaking Plans
Gantt Graphs, Courses of events, and Achievement Diagrams
Normal Updates and Amendments

5.6.2 Advancement Reports and Documentation

Making Customary Advancement Reports
Recording Difficulties and Arrangements
Filing Venture Documentation for Future Reference

5.6.3 Illustrations Learned and Post-Undertaking Documentation

Leading Post-Venture Surveys

Archiving Examples Learned

Further developing Future Task

The board Cycles

5.7 Assessing Task Achievement and Constant Improvement

This part investigates systems for assessing the outcome of an undertaking, gathering input, and carrying out nonstop upgrades.

5.7.1 Key Execution Pointers (KPIs) for Undertaking A good outcome

Estimating Task Courses of events and Achievements

Evaluating Spending plan Adherence and Cost Effectiveness

Partner Fulfillment Measurements

5.7.2 Social occasion Partner Input

Post-Venture Studies and Meetings

Criticism Examination and Execution

Upgrading Correspondence In light of Criticism

5.7.3 Executing Consistent Improvement

Distinguishing Regions for Development

Integrating Illustrations Learned into Future Activities

Developing a Culture of Persistent Improvement

5.8 Taking on Spry Venture the executives

The last piece of this part investigates the standards of Nimble undertaking the executives and its application in designing activities.

5.8.1 Dexterous Systems in Designing

Mixture Task The executives Best Practices

Taking everything into account, Part 5 outfits engineers with the fundamental abilities and techniques for viable undertaking the executives. This chapter provides a comprehensive guide to navigate the complexities of project management in the dynamic field of engineering, from comprehending project lifecycles to adopting agile methodologies and ensuring continuous improvement. Architects will acquire useful bits of knowledge, certifiable models, and noteworthy procedures to effectively lead projects, convey results, and add to the general outcome of their associations.

Part 6: Advancement and Imagination

6.1 Embracing a Culture of Development

Advancement is the main impetus behind progress in designing. This part investigates the significance of encouraging a culture of development inside designing groups and associations.

6.1.1 Characterizing a Culture of Development

Empowering Imagination and Hazard Taking

Establishing a Comprehensive Climate for Thoughts

Perceiving and Compensating Advancement

6.1.2 Position of authority's in Cultivating Advancement

Setting a Dream for Development

Enabling Groups to Examination and Repeat

Separating Progressive Hindrances to Advancement

6.1.3 Advancement Measurements and Key Execution Pointers (KPIs)

Estimating and Evaluating Advancement

Offsetting Momentary Objectives with Long haul Advancement

Gaining from Bombed Developments

6.2 Conceptualizing Strategies

Compelling conceptualizing is a pivotal part of the development interaction. The various methods of brainstorming that can be used to come up with original ideas are discussed in this section.

6.2.1 Customary Meetings to generate new ideas

6.3 Consolidating Configuration Thinking

Configuration believing is a human-focused approach that can start development in designing. This part investigates the standards and use of configuration thinking in designing undertakings.

6.3.1 Sympathy in Plan Thinking

Figuring out End Clients and Partners

Directing Client Exploration and Meetings

Creating Personas for Client Driven Plan

6.3.2 Ideation and Prototyping

Iterative Prototyping and Testing

Co-creation with End Clients

Cooperative Ideation Studios

6.3.3 Carrying out Plan Thinking in Designing Cycles

Incorporating Configuration Thinking with Conventional Designing Strategies

Contextual analyses of Fruitful Plan Thinking in Designing

6.4 Remaining Refreshed on Industry Patterns

Development is intently attached to keeping up to date with the most recent industry patterns and headways. Strategies for trend monitoring and continuous learning are provided in this section.

6.4.1 Industry Distributions and Diaries

Buying into Applicable Diaries and Magazines

Cooperative Understanding Gatherings and Conversations

Online Stages for Industry News

6.4.2 Going to Meetings and Studios

Organizing Valuable open doors at Industry Occasions

Gaining from Featured subject matter experts and Specialists

Exhibiting Creative Ventures at Gatherings

6.4.3 Cooperative Development Stages

Open Development Stages for Information Sharing

Publicly supporting Thoughts and Arrangements

Building a Cooperative Development Environment

6.5 Moral Contemplations in Development

Development should be directed by moral standards. This part investigates the moral contemplations in the development cycle, stressing mindful designing.

6.5.3 Transparency and Accountability in Innovation Communicating Ethical Decisions to Stakeholders Establishing Accountability Mechanisms Learning from Ethical Failures in Innovation

6.6 Sustainability in Engineering Innovation

Considering the Social and Environmental Impact Addressing Ethical Dilemmas in Design Incorporating Ethical Guidelines in Project Planning 6.5.2 Responsible Use of Technology Anticipating and Mitigating Negative Consequences Ethical Considerations in Artificial Intelligence and Automation Collaborating on Ethical Frameworks This segment investigates the joining of manageable practices in the development cycle.

6.6.2 Circular Economy and Waste Reduction Designing for Reusability and Recycling Reducing Waste in Manufacturing Processes Circular Economy Initiatives in Engineering 6.6.3 Corporate Social Responsibility (CSR) in Innovation Incorporating Social Impact Assessments Contributing to Local Communities Reporting and Communicating CSR Efforts 6.7 Future Trends in Engineering Innovation The concluding section of this chapter examines emerging trends, such as Industry 4.0, the Internet of Things (IoT), and collaborative innovation in a globalized.

Section 7: Moral Contemplations in Designing

7.1 Significance of Morals in Designing

This segment lays out the basic job of morals in designing, underlining the effect of moral dynamic on the two people and society.

7.1.1 Characterizing Designing Morals

Grasping the Expert Set of rules

Perceiving the Obligations of Architects

Moral Contemplations in Designing Practice

7.1.2 Cultural Effect of Designing Choices

Offsetting Innovative Headways with Moral Ramifications

The Job of Designers in Open Security

Responsibility and Straightforwardness in Moral Navigation

7.1.3 Contextual analyses in Designing Morals

Analyzing Verifiable Moral Situations in Designing

Gaining from Past Disappointments and Triumphs

The Steadily Advancing Scene of Moral Difficulties

7.2 Moral Dynamic Systems

Designs frequently face complex moral predicaments. This part gives structures to direct moral dynamic in different designing situations.

7.2.1 Utilitarianism in Designing Morals

Gauging the Best Great for the Best Number

7.3 Dependable Exploration and Advancement

This part investigates the moral contemplations implanted in research works on, empowering capable and moral conduct all through the examination cycle.

7.3.1 Moral Rules for Exploration
Educated Assent and Moral Treatment regarding Members
Guaranteeing Information Protection and Secrecy
Tending to Possible Irreconcilable situations

7.3.2 Mindful Direct of Exploration
Respectability in Exploratory Plan and Information Examination
Detailing Exact and Straightforward Outcomes
Tending to Literary theft and Licensed innovation Concerns

7.3.3 Moral Contemplations in Arising Advancements

Bioethics in Biotechnology and Hereditary Designing

Simulated intelligence Morals and Mindful Turn of events

Moral Ramifications of Nanotechnology and High level Materials

7.4 Ecological Morals in Designing

Ecological maintainability is a center part of moral designing. This part digs into the moral contemplations encompassing ecological effect and protection.

7.4.1 Feasible Designing Practices

Limiting Ecological Impression in Plan

Life Cycle Evaluations for Eco-Accommodating Items

7.5 Civil rights and Inclusivity in Designing

Designing tasks can have huge cultural effects. This segment investigates the moral contemplations connected with civil rights, variety, and inclusivity.

7.5.1 Social Obligation in Designing

Tending to Social Imbalances and Inconsistencies

Elevating Admittance to Innovation and Foundation

Local area Commitment and Participatory Plan

7.5.2 Variety and Inclusivity in Designing Groups

Cultivating Comprehensive Workplaces

Separating Boundaries to Passage in the Field

Tending to Predisposition and Segregation in Designing Practices

7.5.3 Moral Contemplations in Human Upgrade Advancements

Offsetting Innovative Headways with Common freedoms

Moral Utilization of Biomedical Upgrades

Cultural Ramifications of Human Expansion

7.6 Moral Administration in Designing

Moral administration is pivotal in directing designing groups and associations. The principles of ethical leadership and their application to the engineering industry are the subject of this section.

7.6.1 Qualities of Moral Forerunners in Designing

Uprightness and Straightforwardness in Direction

Sympathy and Thought for Partner

Government assistance

Showing others how its done in Moral Direct

7.6.2 Advancing Moral Culture in Associations

Creating and Imparting Moral Codes

Laying out Informant Securities

Empowering a Shout out Culture

7.6.3 Settling Moral Contentions in Authority

Adjusting Authoritative Objectives and Moral Contemplations

Looking for Direction from Moral Boards of trustees and Counselors

The Job of Expert Social orders in Moral Authority

7.7 Innovation and Protection Morals

The quick advancement of innovation delivers moral

contemplations connected with protection. This segment investigates the moral components of innovative progressions.

7.7.1 Protection Worries in Information Assortment and Examination

Guaranteeing Informed Assent in Information Assortment

Tending to Predispositions in Information Calculations

Offsetting Mechanical Development with Protection Freedoms

7.7.2 Moral Utilization of Observation Innovations

Adjusting Public Wellbeing and Individual Protection

Legitimate and Moral Contemplations in Reconnaissance

Local area Commitment in Choices In regards to Reconnaissance

7.7.3 Network safety and Moral Hacking

Moral Obligations in Network safety Practices

Shielding Computerized Data and Frameworks

Dependable Revelation in Moral Hacking

7.8 Worldwide Designing Morals

Designs frequently work in a globalized setting, requiring contemplations of social and worldwide moral principles. Global perspectives on engineering ethics are examined in this section.

7.8.1 Social Relativism and Moral Universalism

Exploring Moral Contrasts Across Societies

Creating Culturally diverse Ability in Designing

7.9 Expert Turn of events and Morals Training

The last piece of this part investigates the joining of morals schooling in proficient turn of events, guaranteeing that architects are outfitted with the information and apparatuses to explore moral difficulties.

7.9.1 Morals Training in Designing Educational plans

Coordinating Morals Courses in Scholastic Projects

Case-Based Learning and Moral Issue Conversations

Industry Associations in Morals Schooling

7.9.2 Consistent Moral Preparation for Experts

Participating in Proficient Morals Studios

Online Courses and Proceeding with Schooling in Morals

Genuine Use of Moral Standards

7.9.3 Mentorship and Job

Demonstrating in Moral Turn of events

The Job of Guides in Moral Direction

Proficient Good examples and Moral Administration

Making a Culture of Responsibility and Moral Greatness

All in all, Part 7 gives an extensive investigation of moral contemplations

Part 8: Wellbeing and Prosperity

Part 8: Wellbeing and Prosperity in Designing

8.1 Focusing on Mental and Actual Wellbeing

This part features the significance of focusing on mental and actual prosperity in the requesting field of designing.

8.1.1 Perceiving the Effect of Designing Stressors

Distinguishing Pressure Elements in Designing Work

Tending to Emotional well-being Shame

Significance of Taking care of oneself in High-Stress Conditions

8.1.2 Methodologies for Stress The executives

Carrying out Pressure Help Procedures

Advancing Balance between serious and fun activities

Empowering Standard Severs and Time

8.1.3 Emotional wellness Assets for Designers

Getting to Directing and Backing Administrations

Making a Steady Work environment Culture

Representative Help Projects and Emotional wellness Advantages

8.2 Ergonomics and Actual Wellbeing

This segment investigates the meaning of ergonomics and actual wellbeing for engineers who invest huge energy dealing with PCs and in research facilities.

8.2.1 Planning Ergonomic Work areas

Significance of Legitimate Work area Arrangement and Seat Ergonomics

Lessening Outer muscle Strain

Consolidating Development and Extending Activities

8.2.2 Eye Wellbeing in Designing

Tending to Eye Strain from Screen Time

Executing the 20-20-20 Rule

Customary Eye Assessments and Eye Care Practices

8.2.3 Advancing Actual Wellness

Empowering Customary Work-out Schedules

Work environment Work out regimes and Offices

Integrating Active work into Everyday Schedules

8.3 Sustenance and Dietary Propensities

A fair eating regimen is urgent for supporting energy and concentration. This part stresses the job of nourishment in advancing in general wellbeing for engineers.

8.3.1 Good dieting Propensities

Adjusted Nourishment for Mental Capability

Significance of Normal Feasts and Bites

Hydration and its Effect on Execution

8.3.2 Exploring Dietary Difficulties in Designing Conditions

Defeating Time Requirements for Good dieting

Settling on Informed Food Decisions in Workplaces

Cooperative Nourishment Projects in the Work environment

8.3.3 Tending to Unique Dietary Necessities

Taking special care of Different Dietary Prerequisites

Bringing issues to light and Obliging Dietary Limitations

Making Comprehensive Nourishment Strategies.

8.4 Rest Cleanliness and Quality Rest

Quality rest is primary to by and large prosperity. The significance of good sleep hygiene and methods for getting enough rest are discussed in this section.

8.4.2 Managing Sleep Challenges in Engineering Roles Addressing

Irregular Work Hours and Shifts Strategies for Minimizing Work-Related Sleep Disruptions Seeking Professional Help for Persistent Sleep Issues 8.4.3 Promoting Healthy Sleep Practices in the Workplace Encouraging a Culture of Respect for Sleep Needs Providing Facilities for Rest and Rejuvenation Awareness Programs on the Importance of Sleep

8.5 Building Resilience and Coping Mechanisms

Engineering professionals frequently face challenges Strategies for overcoming stress and building resilience are discussed in this section.

8.5.1 Creating Versatility Notwithstanding Difficulties

8.6 Social Prosperity and Group Elements

Social associations assume a vital part in general prosperity. This segment investigates the significance of social connections and positive group elements.

8.6.1 Sustaining Positive Working environment Connections

Building Trust and Brotherhood Among Colleagues

Observing Triumphs and Achievements Together

Tending to and Settling Group Clashes

8.6.2 Empowering Social Collaboration in the Work environment

Group Building Exercises and Occasions

Open Correspondence Channels for Social Association

Advancing Inclusivity and Variety in Friendly Drives

8.6.3 Steady Authority for Group Prosperity

Pioneers as Supporters for Representative Prosperity

Empowering Open Correspondence About Prosperity

Perceiving and Tending to Burnout in Groups

8.7 Incorporating Prosperity Into Hierarchical Culture

This part investigates techniques for associations to install a culture of prosperity, elevating a comprehensive way to deal with worker wellbeing.

8.7.1 Initiative Obligation to Client

Part 9: Future Patterns in Designing

9.1 Progressions in Computerized reasoning

(artificial intelligence) and AI (ML)

This segment investigates the developing scene of artificial intelligence and ML in designing, looking at their effect on cycles, plan, and advancement.

9.1.1 Reconciliation of simulated intelligence in Designing Plan

Man-made intelligence driven Plan Robotization

Generative Plan and Enhancement

Human-man-made intelligence Joint effort in the Inventive flow

9.1.2 man-made intelligence for Prescient Support and Unwavering quality

Observing Hardware Wellbeing with simulated intelligence

Foreseeing Disappointments and Free time

Upgrading Resource The executives with ML

9.1.3 Moral Contemplations in man-made intelligence and ML

Tending to Predisposition and Decency in Calculations

Straightforwardness and Logic in simulated intelligence Frameworks

Capable simulated intelligence Execution in Designing

9.2 Reasonable and Green Designing Practices

Supportability keeps on being a focal concentration in designing. This segment investigates arising patterns in maintainable and green designing practices.

9.2.1 Round Economy and Shut Circle Frameworks

Planning for Recyclability and Reusability

Limiting Waste in Assembling Cycles

Shutting Asset Circles in Designing Tasks

9.2.2 Environmentally friendly power Advances

Headways in Sunlight based and Wind Power

Energy Capacity and Framework Incorporation

Zap and Manageable Transportation

9.2.3 Eco-Accommodating Materials and Green Development

Supportable Structure Materials

Low-Carbon Development Techniques
Green Foundation for Metropolitan Turn of events

9.3 Web of Things (IoT) and Shrewd Urban areas

The IoT is changing the manner in which urban communities and framework work. This part digs into the job of IoT and savvy advances in molding the fate of designing.

9.3.1 IoT in Infrastructure Management and Monitoring Smart Sensors for Structural Health Monitoring Predictive Analytics for Infrastructure Maintenance IoT Applications in Water and Energy Management 9.3.2 Building Smart and Connected Cities Urban Planning with IoT Data Intelligent Transportation Systems Enhancing

Public Services with IoT 9.3.3 Cybersecurity Challenges in Smart Infrastructure Securing IoT Devices and Networks Privacy Concerns in Smart City Technologies Implementing Resilient Cybersecurity Measures

9.4 Innovations in Biotechnology and Bioengineering

Biotechnology' This segment investigates the crossing point of designing and biotechnology.

9.4.1 Organically Roused Plan Biomimicry in Designing Arrangements Biohybrid Frameworks and Gadgets Saddling Nature for Economical Designing 9.4.2 Biomedical Designing Leap forwards

Progresses in Prosthetics and Inserts

Customized Medication and 3D Bioprinting

Human-Machine Connection points for Wellbeing

9.4.3 Moral Contemplations in Bioengineering

Protection and Security in Biometric Advances

Mindful Utilization of Hereditary Designing

Offsetting Biotechnological Progressions with Moral Rules

9.5 Mechanical technology and Mechanization Patterns

Mechanical technology and robotization are developing quickly. This part investigates the most recent patterns in mechanical advances and their applications in designing.

Guaranteeing Security and Morals in Mechanical Medical services Arrangements

9.6 High level Materials and Nanotechnology

Advancements in materials science are altering designing. The most recent advancements in nanotechnology and advanced materials are examined in this section.

9.6.1 Brilliant and Versatile Materials

Shape Memory Compounds and Polymers

Self-Mending and Self-Fixing Materials

Responsive and Programmable Materials

9.6.2 Nanomaterials and Nanocomposites

Applications in Hardware and Energy Stockpiling

Nanotechnology for Water Purging

Difficulties and Contemplations in Nanomaterial Designing

9.6.3 Natural Effect of Cutting edge Materials

Life Cycle Appraisals for Arising Materials

Green Amalgamation Techniques in Material Science

Administrative Structures for Novel Materials

9.7 Space Investigation and Aviation design

Space investigation is seeing huge headways. This part investigates the patterns in space and advanced plane design.

9.7.1 Business Space Travel and The travel industry

9.8 Information Science and Large Information in Designing

The rising volume of information is reshaping designing practices. This segment investigates the job of information science and enormous information in designing.

9.8.1 Prescient Examination for Support and Enhancement

Information Driven Dynamic in Designing

AI for Example Acknowledgment

Continuous Information Handling in Modern Frameworks

9.8.2 Advanced Twins and Recreation Displaying

Making Virtual Copies of Actual Frameworks

Recreating Certifiable Situations for Testing

Improving Plan and Execution with Advanced Twins

9.8.3 Moral Contemplations in Information Driven Designing

Protection and Security in Information Assortment

Fair and Dependable Utilization of Calculations

Straightforwardness and Responsibility in Information Practices

9.9 Quantum Registering in Designing

Quantum registering holds the possibility to change calculation. This part investigates the arising patterns in quantum registering and its applications in designing.

9.9.1 Quantum Figuring Standards

Quantum Pieces (Qubits) and Superposition

Quantum Snare for Improved Handling

Quantum Calculations for Designing Critical thinking

9.9.2 Utilizations of Quantum Registering in Designing

Streamlining Complex Frameworks and Calculations

Quantum Cryptography for Upgraded Security

Quantum AI in Designing Examination

9.9.3 Difficulties and Future Possibilities in Quantum Designing

Conquering Quantum Decoherence

Versatility and Incorporation of Quantum Frameworks

Cooperative Innovative work in Quantum Designing

9.10 The Fate of Designing Instruction

This part investigates the advancing scene of designing schooling, taking into account imaginative methodologies and innovations.

9.10.1 On the web and Mixed Learning in Designing

Progressions in Virtual Research centers and Recreations

Cooperative Web-based Stages for Designing Training

Long lasting Learning and Persistent Expert Turn of events

9.10.2 Interdisciplinary and Undertaking Based Learning

Separating Customary Storehouses in Designing Schooling

Industry Coordinated effort in Task Based Learning.

Appendix: Glossary of Designing Terms

This glossary gives definitions to key designing terms to help perusers in grasping specialized ideas and phrasing.

Algorithm: A bit by bit methodology or recipe for taking care of an issue or achieving an errand.

Biomimicry: The plan and creation of materials, designs, and frameworks that are designed according to natural elements and cycles.

Computer aided design (PC Supported Plan): The utilization of PC frameworks to aid the creation, change, investigation, or improvement of a plan.

Cobot (Cooperative Robot): A robot intended to work close by people in a common work area, upgrading cooperation and effectiveness.

Information Science: The field of study that includes separating experiences and information from information through different strategies, including insights, AI, and information examination.

Advanced Twin: A virtual portrayal of an actual item or framework, giving constant information and experiences for checking, examination, and reenactment.

Entropy: A proportion of the issue or haphazardness in a framework, frequently utilized in thermodynamics and data hypothesis.

Hereditary Designing: The control of a creature's qualities utilizing biotechnology to accomplish positive characteristics or results.

Human-Machine Point of interaction (HMI): The place of connection between a human and a machine, frequently through a graphical UI or contact screen.

IoT: Internet of Things The organization of interconnected gadgets and frameworks that convey and impart information to one another.

AI: A subset of man-made reasoning that empowers PCs to learn and further develop execution without unequivocal programming.

Nanotechnology: The control of issue at the nanoscale, frequently including materials or designs with aspects of 1 to 100 nanometers.

Optimization: The most common way of making a framework or plan as compelling or practical as could be expected, frequently including expanding or limiting specific boundaries.

Photonics: The review and use of light to produce, control, and distinguish signals, ordinarily as lasers and optics.

Quantum Processing: A sort of figuring that utilizes standards of quantum mechanics, like superposition and snare, to perform computations.

Resilience: The capacity of a framework or material to recuperate and adjust subsequent to encountering pressure, shocks, or unsettling influences.

Reasonable Designing: The act of planning and executing frameworks, items, and cycles that limit natural effect and advance long haul reasonability.

Telemedicine: The utilization of broadcast communications innovation to give medical care benefits from a distance, working with finding, interview, and therapy.

Metropolitan Preparation: The planning and arrangement of urban spaces, including transportation, infrastructure, and land use, to